THE HUMAN MACHINE

THE *OUTER SHELL*

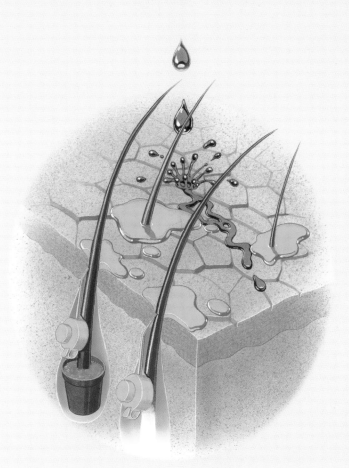

Sarah Angliss

Illustrations by Graham Rosewarne

Thameside Press

U.S. publication copyright © 2000 Thameside Press.
International copyright reserved in all countries.
No part of this book may be reproduced in any
form without written permission from the publisher.

Distributed in the United States by
Smart Apple Media
123 South Broad Street
Mankato, Minnesota 56001

Text copyright © Sarah Angliss 2000

Editor: Susie Brooks
Designer: Helen James
Educational consultant: Carol Ballard

Printed in Singapore

ISBN 1-929298-21-8
Library of Congress Catalog Card Number 99-66187

10 9 8 7 6 5 4 3 2 1

Words in **bold** are explained in the glossary on pages 30 and 31.

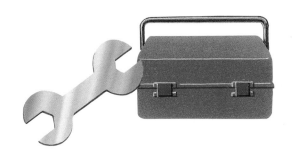

CONTENTS

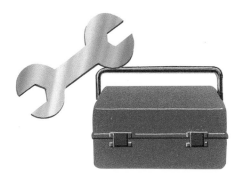

THE OUTER SHELL

Think of your body as an amazing machine—a human machine. It's packed with parts that need to keep working wherever you are. That's why you have your outer shell. This casing of skin and hair protects the inside of your body and adjusts to suit the conditions around you.

Super shell

Your outer shell is adapting all the time to keep your body working properly. Your skin, for example, stretches like a sheet of rubber to let you move. Its outer layers can darken to protect your insides from the rays of the Sun. As your outer shell is almost completely sealed, it also helps to keep out dirt and germs—and to stop your inner body parts from slopping out.

4

Likely looks?

Every outer shell works in roughly the same way, but each one looks unique. The way someone looks on the outside is called their appearance. It helps us to tell who they are.

We know that people don't really look like the figures in the diagram below! The main pictures in this book are drawn with a little imagination. But look at each one carefully—they show you what your outer shell can do and how different parts of it work.

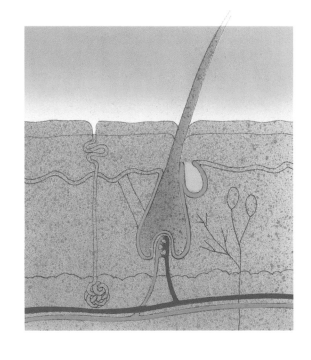

Real feel

Look for pictures like the one above throughout this book. They show which parts of your outer shell are discussed on each page, and give you an idea of what they really look like.

Breakdown!

Just like the casing of any other machine, your outer shell needs looking after. Although skin can repair itself, it may sometimes be damaged so badly it needs a helping hand. Toolboxes like this one show a few of the things that can go wrong with your outer shell—and how you can help to keep it in good condition.

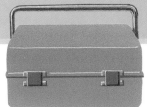

5

SHRINK WRAP

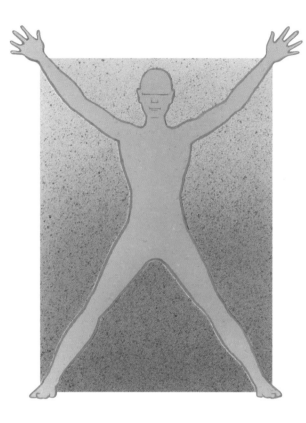

Most ordinary machines, such as computers and toasters, come in rigid, lifeless cases. But a human is held together inside a stretchy layered wrapping that's alive—your skin.

Your skin is the largest working part of your body. Laid out flat, it would cover up to 30 pages of this book.

Living layers

The building blocks of your skin are tiny units called **cells** that lock together like tiles. The outer part of your skin is called your **epidermis**. Its surface is hard and dead, but soft new living cells are forming all the time underneath.

The layer of skin below your epidermis is called your **dermis**. This has many working parts, including hair **follicles**, **sweat glands**, **sebaceous glands**, **blood vessels**, **nerves**, and tiny muscles. These all work together, protecting everything inside you, keeping your body at the right temperature, and helping you to feel and adapt to your surroundings.

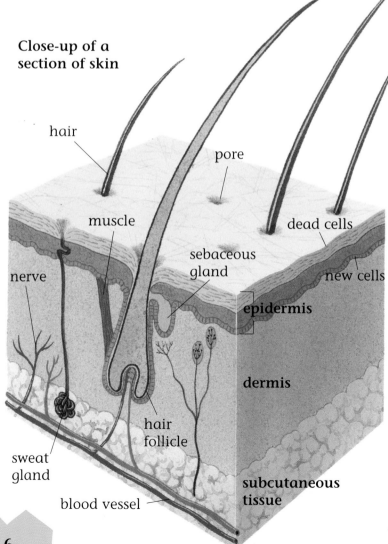

Close-up of a section of skin

hair

pore

muscle

dead cells

sebaceous gland

new cells

nerve

epidermis

dermis

hair follicle

sweat gland

blood vessel

subcutaneous tissue

Skin prints

The papillae of your dermis form tiny ridges. The grooves between them are deepest on your palms and soles, where your skin is thickest. These are the places where you can see the ridges most clearly. Papillae form the patterns that create your fingerprints. These depend mainly on your **genes** (see pages 22-23).

Rapid repairs

*The human outer shell isn't completely scratchproof— but it can heal itself if it is slightly grazed or torn. If you scrape off some skin cells, new ones will grow rapidly to take their place. A slight graze can disappear altogether in just a few days. But a deeper cut or serious burn may leave a permanent mark on your skin. This is called a **scar**.*

Flexible fibers

The dermis is soft and jelly-like. It's largely made up of crisscrossing **fibers** of a stretchy material called **elastin**. This makes your skin slightly elastic, just like a sheet of rubber. Elastin is a **protein**. Another protein in your skin, called **collagen**, is very tough. It helps to keep your skin strong and supple.

The top of your dermis and bottom of your epidermis are covered in tiny nodules called **papillae**. These act like the bumps on a nonslip mat, holding your epidermis firmly in place.

Inner insulation

A loose, fatty layer at the bottom of the dermis fixes your skin to the body muscles underneath. This layer, called **subcutaneous tissue**, helps to **insulate** your skin. It makes it harder for heat inside your body to pass through to your epidermis, where it can be lost into the air around you.

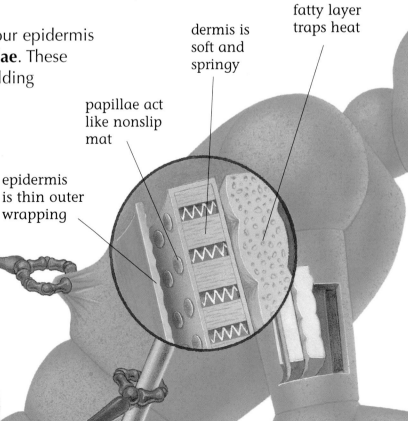

fatty layer traps heat

dermis is soft and springy

papillae act like nonslip mat

epidermis is thin outer wrapping

WEAR AND REPAIR

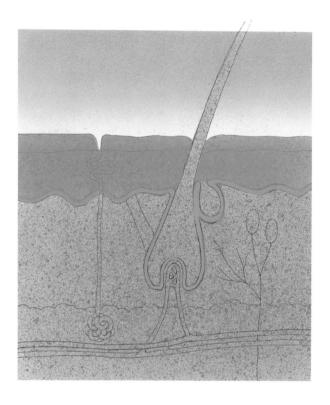

Skin gets so much wear and tear, it needs to keep repairing and renewing itself. Some parts of your body get scuffed far more than others—so they have thicker, tougher, faster-growing skin.

old dead cells flake off skin's surface

Shedding skin

The deepest layer of your **epidermis** is constantly forming new **cells**. As they grow, they flatten the cells above them and push them toward the surface. There is no blood flowing through the epidermis, so its cells have no supply of the **nutrients** they need to survive. That's why they die as they are pushed further away from the **dermis**. A horny material, called **keratin**, forms in the cells as they die. This makes them hard and tough.

Just dust

When you dust your home, you're probably sweeping away scraps of your epidermis. Lots of the dust around you is made up of dead skin cells. Dry skin flakes off more easily than moist skin. If you burn yourself—in sunlight for instance—your epidermis may peel off in large, thin patches.

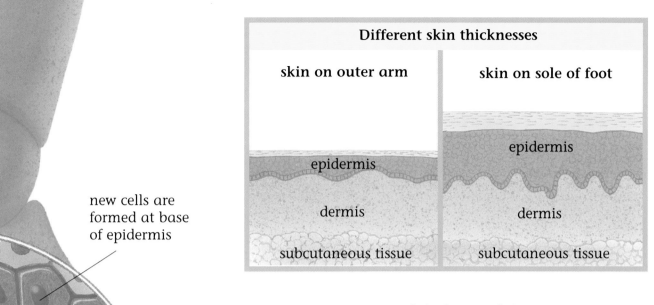

Different skin thicknesses

skin on outer arm	skin on sole of foot
epidermis	epidermis
dermis	dermis
subcutaneous tissue	subcutaneous tissue

new cells are
formed at base
of epidermis

new cells
push old ones
outward

Thick 'n thin

Some areas of your body get more wear than others—that's why the thickness of your skin varies. The skin on the palms of your hands, for example, is about ten times thicker than the skin on your eyelids. And the soles of your feet are thicker still. Walking around barefoot can be painful at first—but the more you do it, the tougher your soles become.

Tough stuff

Your body sheds thousands of dead cells every minute—millions when you rub yourself with a rough towel. Shoes and clothes wear thin if they are constantly rubbed. But if a patch of skin gets scuffed a lot, it will grow a thicker epidermis. This toughens it up so it can last a lifetime.

Lumping it

If your skin is rubbed badly or burned, you may end up with a blister. A blister forms when the damaged area below the skin's surface fills with a watery fluid and a bubble appears on top. Badly fitting shoes often cause blisters because they rub harshly against parts of your foot.

PROTECTIVE COAT

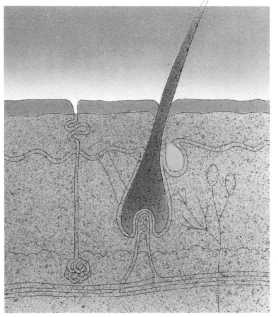

The human outer shell acts like a built-in raincoat. It can keep out dirt and germs as well as water. Your skin also stops you from drying out as it locks in some of your body's moisture.

Waterproof walls

The **cells** of your **epidermis** overlap like roof tiles, forming a barrier that stops water from entering your body. The **keratin** that makes the outer layers of your epidermis hard also makes them waterproof. Keratin acts like the glazing on tiles, stopping too much water from soaking through the outer cells into deeper layers of skin.

Slippery surface

Your skin has a light coating of oil, just like a waxed jacket. This comes from a set of juice-makers, called **sebaceous glands**, that are buried in your **dermis**. A few of these glands squirt oil directly on to your skin, but most are linked to hair **follicles**. Their oil coats the hairs that are developing under the surface of your skin.

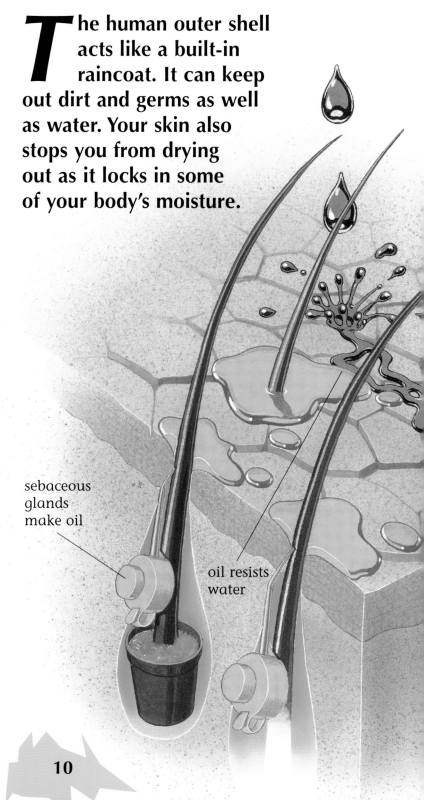

sebaceous glands make oil

oil resists water

How a spot forms

If a sebaceous gland produces too much oil, it may become blocked. The pocket that carries the oil will stretch, forming a spot. If the opening of a sebaceous gland clogs up, the oil may dry and darken, forming a **blackhead**. Spots can spread if the oil in a blocked gland—or the area around it—is infected by germs.

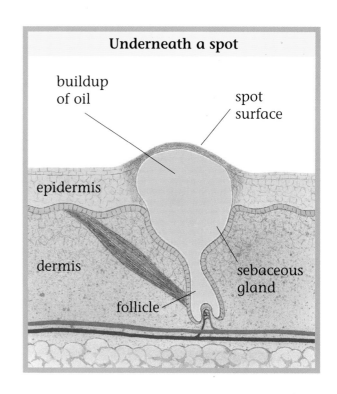

Underneath a spot

buildup of oil

spot surface

epidermis

dermis

sebaceous gland

follicle

Germ-busting

Sebaceous oil doesn't only keep your skin and hair waterproof. It also contains chemicals that act like mild disinfectants, helping to kill some of the germs lurking on the outside of your body. Your overlapping skin cells act as a barrier that keeps many germs locked out.

skin cells overlap like tiles

water runs off skin surface

Find out more about sebaceous glands and oil on page 17.

Locked in

About seven-tenths of your body is made up of water. Your skin acts like the plastic wrap around bread or cheese, locking in most of this moisture. It helps to keep the amount of water inside you finely balanced.

Waterlogged

There are very few sebaceous glands on the palms of your hands and the soles of your feet. That's why lots more water can get under the skin of these parts of your body. When you have a long soak in the bath, the skin that covers your palms and soles can take in so much water it goes wrinkly. But as soon as it dries, your skin becomes smooth again.

SUPER SENSORS

Your outer shell is covered with sensors that help you to keep in touch with the world around you. They let you feel pressure, texture, pain, heat, or cold.

nerves carry messages to brain

sensors near surface feel light touch

Fine feelers

The **sensors** in your skin are at the ends of long **fibers** called **nerves**. These act like a network of wires, linking your skin to your brain. When something triggers a sensor in your skin, electrical pulses travel along your nerves to your brain. These messages let you know that you've felt something.

Separate signals

The simplest sensors in your skin are bare nerve endings near the surface. These give you signals of pain. You have lots of them so your body can tell when it's in danger. Other more complex bundles of nerve endings help you to feel texture, temperature, or pressure. If these are triggered strongly, they may also feel pain.

Scratch it

Scratching is an instant way to relieve an itch because it makes it harder for a tickling feeling to reach your brain. When you scratch yourself, your nerves have to carry mild pain signals. This makes them too busy to carry the messages that make you feel itchy.

Varied vibes

Some areas of skin contain far more nerve endings than others. This makes them much more sensitive. Your fingertips, for example, are packed with sensors that are only a fraction of an inch apart, enabling them to feel the slightest touch. Your thighs are far less sensitive as their nerve endings can be around two inches apart.

Take a look at the diagram below. It looks out of proportion because some of the most sensitive body parts have been drawn extra large in size.

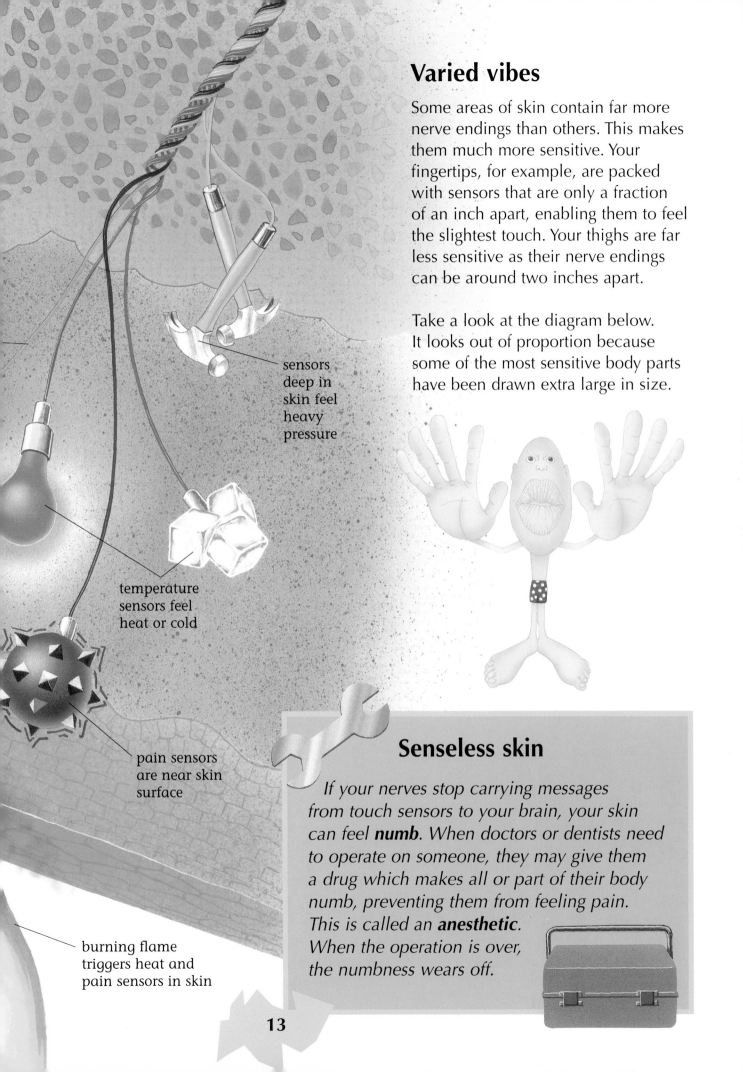

sensors deep in skin feel heavy pressure

temperature sensors feel heat or cold

pain sensors are near skin surface

burning flame triggers heat and pain sensors in skin

Senseless skin

If your nerves stop carrying messages from touch sensors to your brain, your skin can feel **numb***. When doctors or dentists need to operate on someone, they may give them a drug which makes all or part of their body numb, preventing them from feeling pain. This is called an* **anesthetic***. When the operation is over, the numbness wears off.*

TEMPERATURE CONTROL

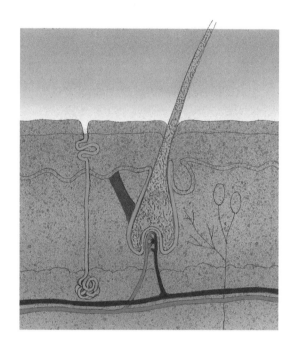

Heat loss from your body

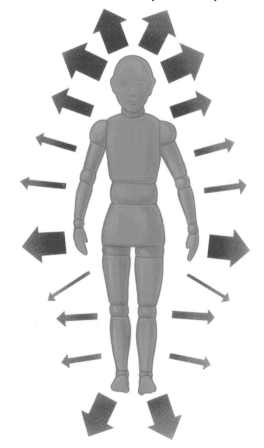

The human machine will only work within a narrow range of temperatures. Your outer shell helps to make sure you don't become too hot or too cold.

A healthy body has an inner temperature of around 98.6°F. Like a perfectly heated room, it stays this way, no matter what the conditions are like outside. Your body's ability to keep the same temperature is called **homeostasis**.

Cool down

If you start to get too hot, your skin springs into action. **Blood vessels** in your **dermis** widen, letting more of your warm blood flow closer to the surface. Like the water in a radiator, your blood will let some of its heat escape into the cooler air around you. This helps to lower your body temperature.

Radiation rate

On a cold day, some parts of your body lose more heat than others. Your feet, ears, and hands, for instance, lose lots of heat, especially if they're uncovered. That's because more blood flows to the skin around these parts. As more blood nears the surface, more heat is lost to the air outside.

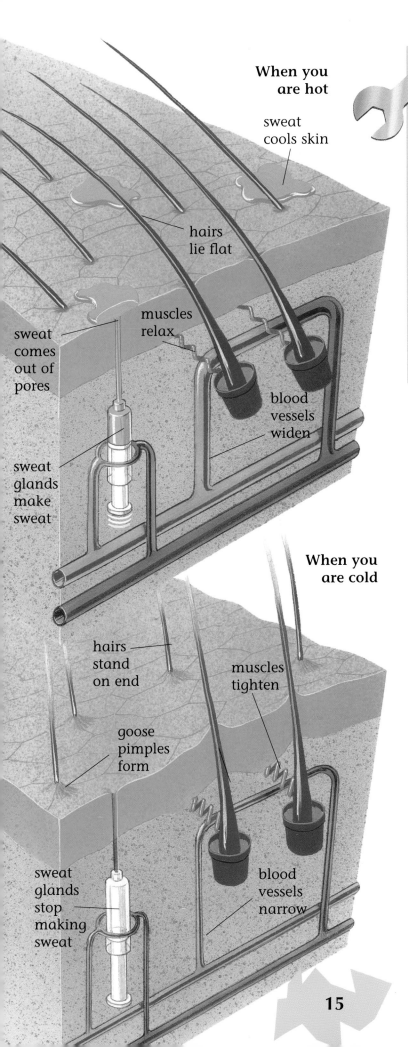

When you are hot

sweat cools skin

hairs lie flat

muscles relax

sweat comes out of pores

sweat glands make sweat

blood vessels widen

When you are cold

hairs stand on end

muscles tighten

goose pimples form

sweat glands stop making sweat

blood vessels narrow

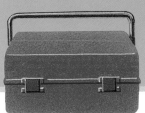

Hot headed

On very hot days, some people sweat so much, they lose too much water and salt from their body. This makes them dizzy and sick—a problem called **heatstroke***. You can avoid heat stroke by drinking plenty of water and avoiding too much exercise on very hot days.*

Letting off steam

Your skin also cools you like a damp towel. When you're hot, thousands of **glands** make a salty juice called **sweat**. This liquid trickles out through tiny holes, called **pores**, on to the surface of your skin. As it **evaporates**, sweat takes heat away from your body.

Warm up

When you're too cold, your skin turns into a heat trap. Blood vessels in your dermis narrow, cutting off some of the blood supply to your skin. As less blood flows close to the surface of your body, you lose less of your heat.

At the same time, tiny muscles in your dermis pull on your body hairs to make them stand up. An animal's thick fur traps warm air close to the skin in this way. But your body hairs are so fine, all they do is make tiny bumps, known as **goose pimples**, appear on your skin.

SPROUTING SHOOTS

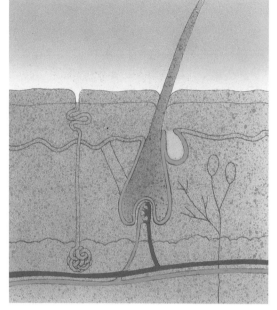

Almost all of the human machine is covered in a mesh of strong, bending hairs. There are different types of hair for different body parts.

Very few areas of your skin are completely hairless. Most people have some sprouting shoots all over their bodies, except on their palms, soles, and lips.

Wonder wig

Hair doesn't only look good—it's also fairly useful. The hair on your head, for example, keeps in heat by trapping pockets of warm air. The **pubic hair** you develop as a teenager is a natural sieve, keeping out grime. Your eyelashes do a similar job, protecting your eyes from dust in the air.

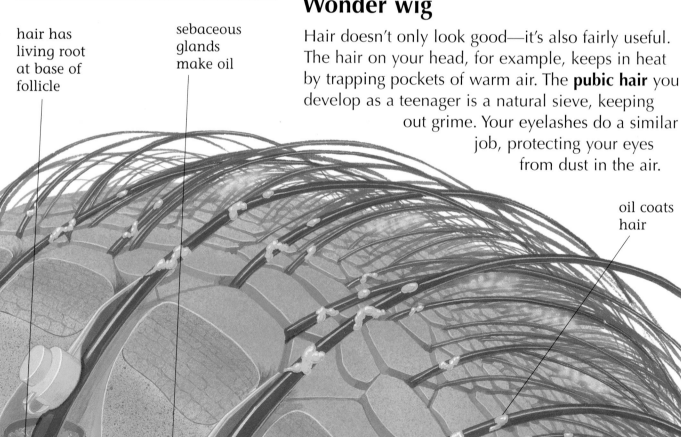

hair has living root at base of follicle

sebaceous glands make oil

oil coats hair

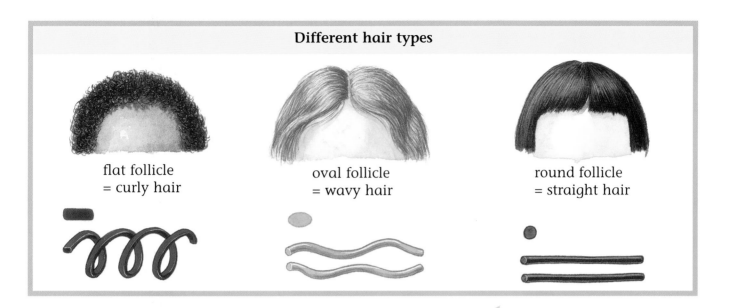

Different hair types

flat follicle
= curly hair

oval follicle
= wavy hair

round follicle
= straight hair

Taking shape

Each hair is formed from **cells** that grow at the bottom of a tiny tube, or **follicle**. The shape of the follicle affects your hair type. Flat follicles force hair to curl, oval ones make it wavy, and round ones let it grow straight. Large follicles give you thick hair, while small ones make it fine.

Follicles are buried in the **dermis** of your skin, where they are linked to tiny **blood vessels**. As new hair cells develop, they push older ones further up toward the surface. Hair cells die as they are pushed away from the follicle's blood supply. They also harden, like skin cells, because the horny material **keratin** forms inside them.

Dead or alive?

Even though your hair is dead, it can look shiny and healthy. That's because each hair has a **sebaceous gland** at its root, providing it with its own oil supply. The oil coats the hair as it grows, keeping it supple. Too much oil can make your hair greasy; too little leaves it dry and brittle.

hairs can trap
pockets of air

Hair raising

Everyone's hair grows at a different rate. But on average we sprout about half an inch of new hair every month. Each hair lives for just a few years. Then it falls out. You lose about 100 hairs a day in this way, but they are usually replaced with new ones.

Bareheaded

*Some men and women have very little hair on their head, and a few have no hair at all. This is often because they have an imbalance of **hormones**—the chemicals that control how their bodies work. Some people cover their baldness with wigs, but others don't mind it at all.*

SCRAPERS

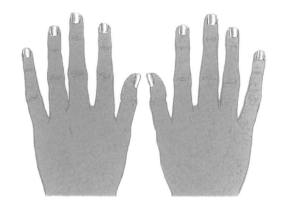

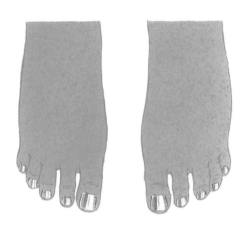

Most of your outer shell is fleshy or hairy. But your nails are hard and tough. These safety shields for your fingers and toes are also your body's scrapers.

Although you normally use tools to scratch and scour things, your nails are your natural scrapers. Unlike most scrapers you make or buy, each nail can last you a lifetime. That's because a nail grows back as fast as it wears away.

New for old

Just like hairs, your nails are made from a crop of skin **cells** that die and harden with **keratin**.

Nail cells develop from a living root, hidden under a fold of skin called the **cuticle**. The white, moon-shaped part at the base of your nail is where most of these cells divide. This is called the **lunula**. As cells form and harden, they push older ones out toward the tip of the finger or toe. Grooves alongside the nail act as guiderails that make sure it grows in the right direction.

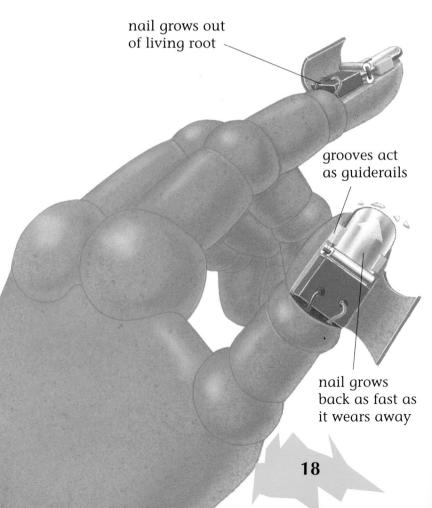

nail grows out of living root

grooves act as guiderails

nail grows back as fast as it wears away

18

Tough touch

Your nails themselves have no feeling. But the skin underneath them—called the **nail bed**—is very sensitive. That's because it's full of **nerve** endings that are triggered by heat, cold, or pressure. Your nails act like tough shields, protecting the tips of your fingers and toes. They also support your fingertips when you pick things up.

Looking healthy

The nail bed has a rich blood supply. This can be seen faintly through your nails, giving them a pinkish tinge. Good-looking nails are a signal that you are healthy. As nails grow so rapidly, they can quickly show signs of illness. If someone isn't eating properly, for example, they may develop oddly shaped nails. Their nails will often become pitted if they are short of **iron**. Bluish nails could mean bad **circulation**.

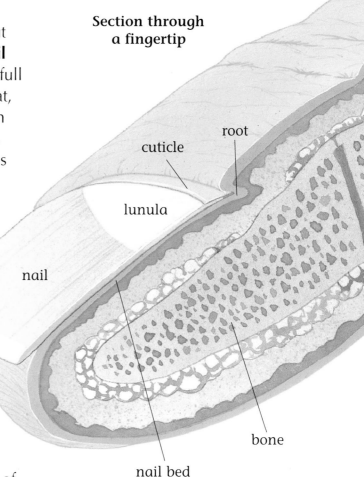

Section through a fingertip

cuticle

root

lunula

nail

bone

nail bed

Growing in

If you don't regularly cut your nails, they may start growing into the nail groove. Ingrown nails can be very painful. Sometimes they may even need to be removed by surgery. Most ingrown nails form on people's toes. They are often caused by tight socks or shoes, which stop the nails growing properly.

Fast growth

Every month, a fingernail grows about two tenths of an inch. In a year, it would grow as long as your little finger if it didn't wear away. In a lifetime, you grow 13 to 16 feet of new nail for every finger and toe. Nails usually grow quicker in the summer than in winter time.

PAINTWORK

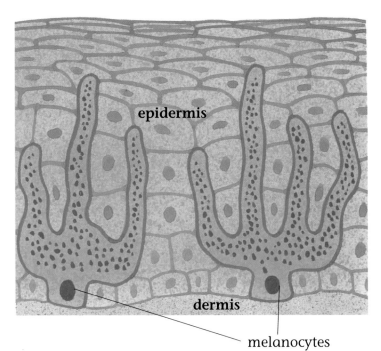

epidermis

dermis

melanocytes

*L*ike the casing of many other machines, the human outer shell can come in different colors. Your body paint is a special chemical called pigment.

If you look around, you'll notice that many people have skin that's a different color from your own. Some may be darker, paler, yellower, or more freckled, for instance.

Creating colors

Your coloring comes from a **pigment** called **melanin**. Melanin is made in special **cells** called **melanocytes**, found in the deepest layer of your **epidermis**. The shade of your skin depends on how much melanin these cells make. People with lots of melanin have dark skin. Those with less have paler skin. Another pigment, called **carotene**, can give the skin a yellowish tinge.

What makes most people's outer shells so different? Find out on pages 22-23.

melanocytes give off pigment into surrounding cells

Pigment palette

Pigment also colors your hair and eyes. Hair pigments are black, red, and yellow. Mixtures of these give many shades, from blond or auburn to brown or black. Your eye color depends on melanin. Blue eyes have less of it than brown eyes.

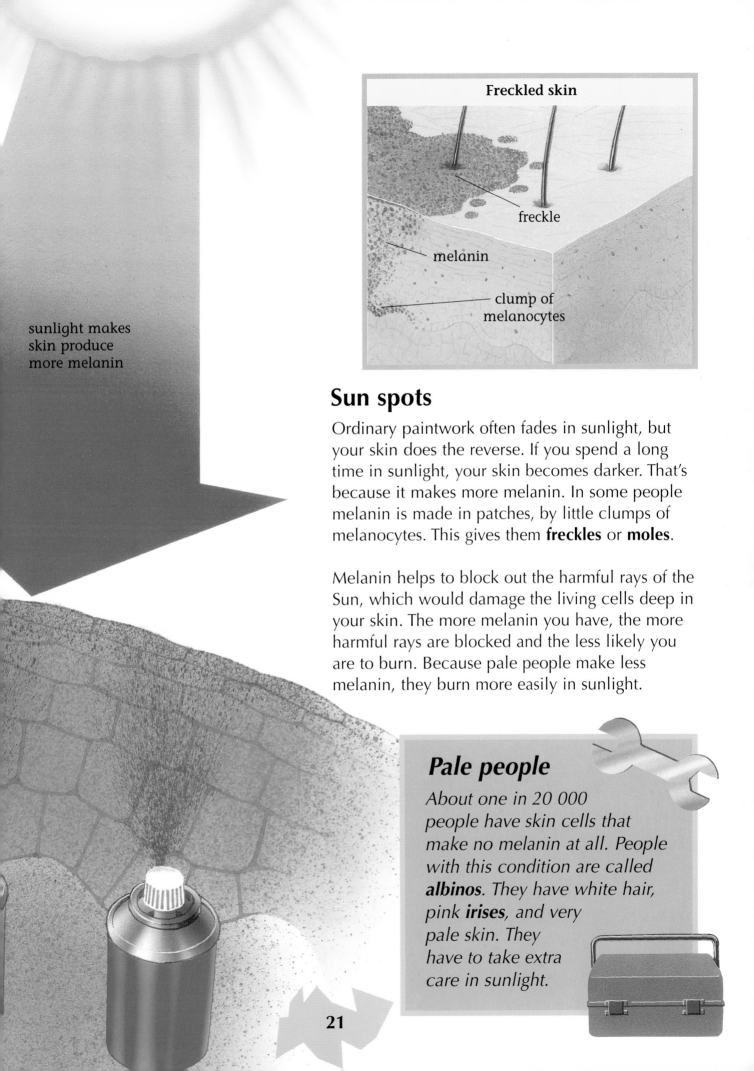

Freckled skin

freckle

melanin

clump of
melanocytes

sunlight makes
skin produce
more melanin

Sun spots

Ordinary paintwork often fades in sunlight, but your skin does the reverse. If you spend a long time in sunlight, your skin becomes darker. That's because it makes more melanin. In some people melanin is made in patches, by little clumps of melanocytes. This gives them **freckles** or **moles**.

Melanin helps to block out the harmful rays of the Sun, which would damage the living cells deep in your skin. The more melanin you have, the more harmful rays are blocked and the less likely you are to burn. Because pale people make less melanin, they burn more easily in sunlight.

Pale people

*About one in 20 000 people have skin cells that make no melanin at all. People with this condition are called **albinos**. They have white hair, pink **irises**, and very pale skin. They have to take extra care in sunlight.*

21

BODY BLUEPRINT

Every human outer shell is made of roughly the same ingredients—but each one looks unique. Your appearance depends largely on your own built-in instructions.

Keep it in the family

If you compare yourself with the rest of your family, you'll probably notice some similarities. That's because each of your body **cells** contains a set of chemicals, called **genes**, which you inherited from your parents. Genes form your body's blueprint—they help to decide how every part of you will grow and work.

Half your genes come from your mother and half from your father. That's why you usually have a mixture of characteristics from both parents. The way these genes mix and match happens by chance.

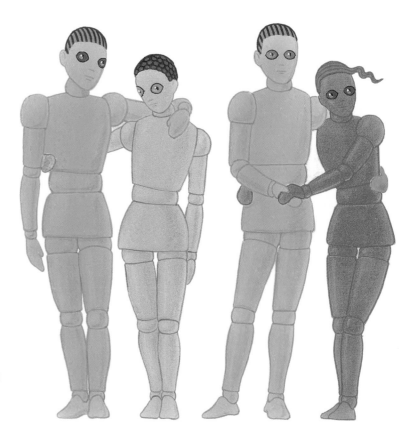

parents A   parents B

Mending the code

Very rarely, people are born with life-threatening diseases because they have a faulty set of genes. Scientists today are learning to decode and mend genes that cause problems. In the future, the treatments they develop could help to save many lives.

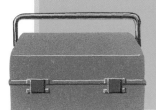

Brown or blue?

Some features of your outer shell, such as the color of your eyes or hair, are decided by one **dominant gene**. A gene giving brown eyes, for example, will overrule a gene giving blue eyes. If you inherit a brown-eyed gene from one of your parents and a blue-eyed gene from the other, your eyes will be brown.

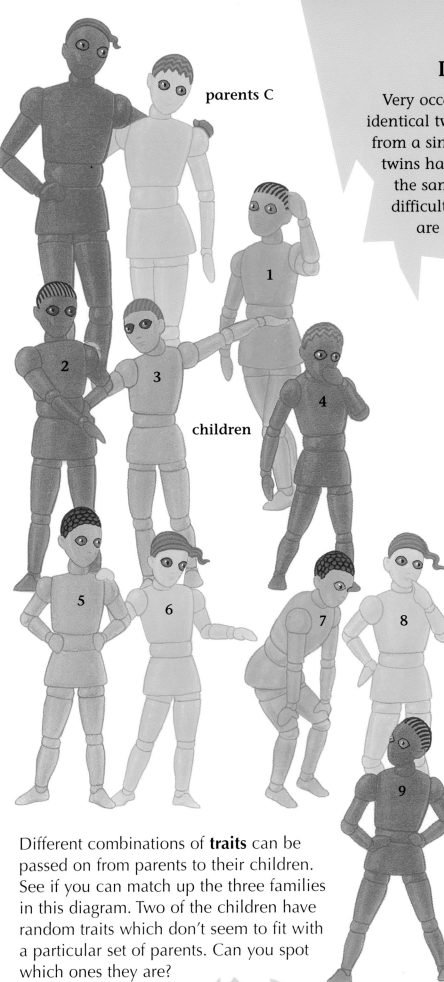

Identical twins

Very occasionally a couple produces identical twins—two babies that develop from a single egg and **sperm**. Identical twins have identical genes. They are the same sex, and it is often very difficult to tell them apart as they are alike in so many ways.

Choice and change

Genes aren't the only things that determine how you look. The life you lead also affects your outer shell. You don't inherit the length or style of your hair, for example—that depends on choices you make.

Most traits, such as height and weight, are decided by a mixture of genes and choices. In general, if your parents are tall, you are more likely to grow tall yourself. But the amount you exercise, the food you eat, and the illnesses you have will also affect the way you develop.

parents C

children

Different combinations of **traits** can be passed on from parents to their children. See if you can match up the three families in this diagram. Two of the children have random traits which don't seem to fit with a particular set of parents. Can you spot which ones they are?

Matching the families

child 1: parents B
child 2: parents B
child 3: random traits
child 4: parents C
child 5: random traits
child 6: parents C
child 7: parents A
child 8: parents C
child 9: parents B

RUNNING DOWN

Although the human outer shell can repair and renew itself, it won't look the same forever. As people grow old, they start to show a few signs of wear.

Signs of age

If you want to judge how old someone is, you may look at their skin and hair. These parts often show telltale signs of aging. Age doesn't change only your appearance—it also affects the way your skin works.

Hair wear

As people grow older, their **cells** start to slow down their work on everyday tasks. One thing they stop doing is producing so much **pigment**. This doesn't only make people's skin paler—it may also cause their hair to lose its color, turning it gray. Many people's hair becomes thinner too, because the blood supply to its roots weakens and the **follicles** die.

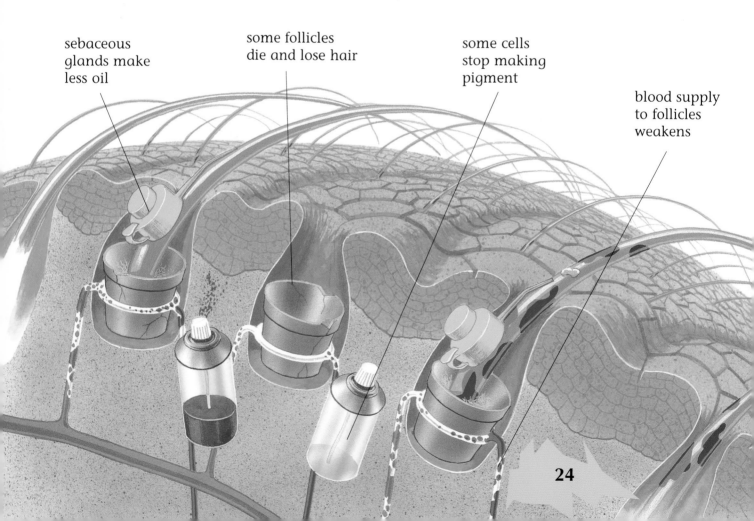

sebaceous glands make less oil

some follicles die and lose hair

some cells stop making pigment

blood supply to follicles weakens

24

Stopping the clock

Genes almost certainly play a part in the aging process. But scientists have found that genes show wear and tear too. As you grow older, the bundles that your genes are clumped in begin to fray, just like rope ends. Some researchers hope to find a way of stopping this fraying process, making many signs of aging a thing of the past.

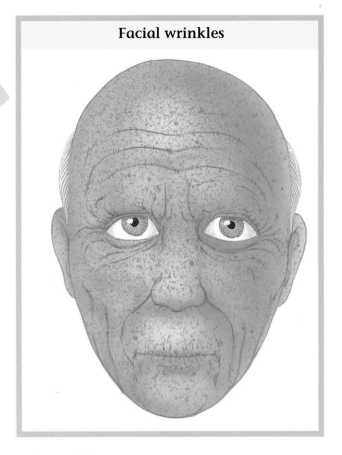

Facial wrinkles

Less stretch

Aging skin loses some of its stretchy **fibers**. This makes it thinner and less elastic, causing it to wrinkle and loosen. Old people's skin also takes longer to heal when it is cut or bruised.

Slowing down

There are many less visible changes that result from aging too. **Sweat glands**, for instance, become far less active, muscles weaken, and **circulation** becomes more sluggish. This makes it harder for skin to control body heat. That's why older people have to take more care about keeping themselves warm or cool.

hair appears thinner and drier

Time lines

Wrinkles appear along the creases where your skin folds as you move it. On your face, they form mainly around your eyes, mouth, and forehead—the parts that move most when you smile or frown.

Old before time

*Some people age quicker than others. Many things can speed up aging, including lifestyle. Smokers often go wrinkly much earlier than the rest of us. That's because the cigarette smoke they breathe in breaks down the stretchy **elastin** in their skin.*

CARE AND SERVICING

Your outer shell has to protect you for a lifetime, so you need to treat it well. Good care and servicing lets you get the best from the blueprint that nature gave you.

A healthy appearance is usually a sign of a healthy body. Just as your outer shell shows traces of age, it can also let you know if there's something wrong on the inside. There are many ways you can help to keep your skin, hair, and nails healthy.

Signs of sickness

When people are unwell, they often look pale or blotchy. Many diseases, such as measles or chicken pox, show themselves as rashes on the skin. A rash can also be a sign of an **allergy** or irritation. Creams and ointments are often used to soothe itches and clear up problems like this.

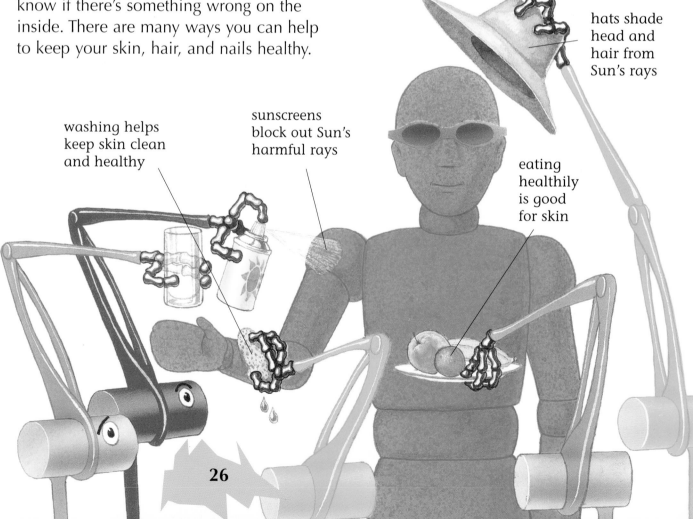

hats shade head and hair from Sun's rays

washing helps keep skin clean and healthy

sunscreens block out Sun's harmful rays

eating healthily is good for skin

New skin

If a large area of skin is very badly damaged, it may not be able to heal itself. But doctors can usually help by planting a new piece of skin over the wound. This operation is called a **skin graft**. The new skin may have been taken from another part of the body, or it could have been grown from a few other skin cells. In time, the grafted skin grows over the damaged area and repairs it.

Clean coat

Everyone should wash their outer shell regularly to keep it fresh and smelling good. Washing stops many everyday germs from entering your body. It also helps to remove oil, **sweat**, and dead surface cells from your skin and hair.

Sun sense

Sunlight is good for your body in fairly small doses—your skin uses it to make **vitamin D**, a chemical that helps you to grow healthy bones. But too much sunlight can burn the skin, making it sore, blistered, and more likely to wrinkle. Sunburn can also increase the risk of skin **cancer**. It's a good idea to limit how long you expose your skin to sunlight—and always use a **sunscreen** to block out the Sun's damaging rays.

Eating well

Your skin, hair, and nails are constantly taking **nutrients** from the food you eat to form new **cells**. Eating a **balanced diet** and drinking plenty of water will help these cells to grow and stay healthy.

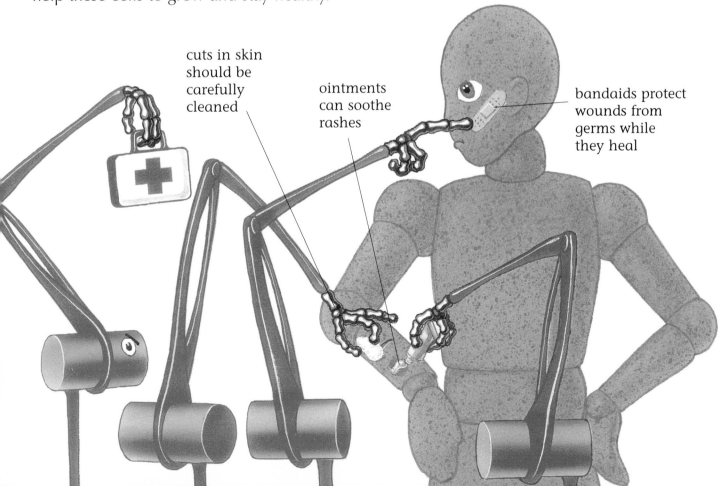

cuts in skin should be carefully cleaned

ointments can soothe rashes

bandaids protect wounds from germs while they heal

OTHER MODELS

Your skin and hair form a perfect wrapping for your body. But some animals have very different coats. Here are some of the other outer shells around.

Crafty chameleons

Chameleons are reptiles that can change the color of their skin to match their surroundings. This **camouflage** makes them very hard to spot. By blending in, chameleons can sneak up on creatures they want to eat—and they can hide from other animals that are on the lookout for a meal.

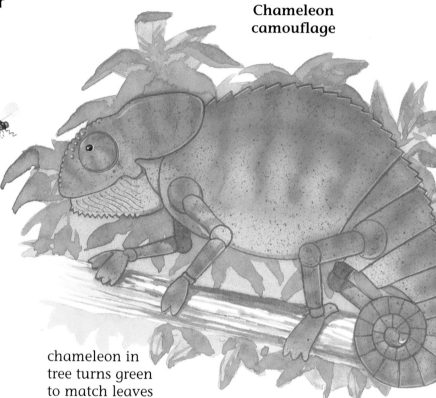

Chameleon camouflage

chameleon in tree turns green to match leaves

Feathered friends

Instead of hairs, birds are covered in feathers. A fluffy layer close to their skin acts like a vest, keeping them warm. Water birds, such as ducks, make extra waterproofing oils in their skin. They often comb their feathers with their beaks, to spread the oils around. The oil stops their feathers from being weighed down by the water and helps to keep their bodies warm and dry underneath.

chameleon in desert turns brown to match sandy rock

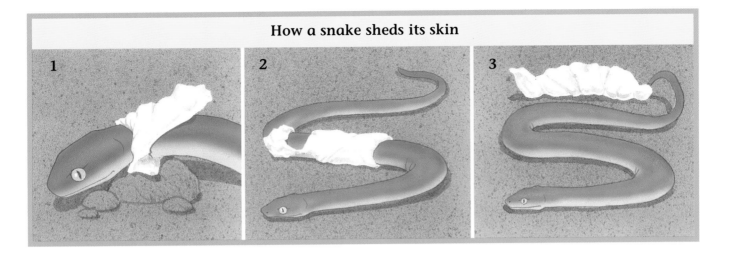

1
2
3

Slippery snakes

A snake is covered in scales that are made of **keratin**, just like your nails and hair. Scales form a tough wrapping around the snake's body. But this outer shell isn't stretchy or flaky like yours. As a snake grows, it has to shed its skin all in one go. To do this, the snake rubs its head against a branch or rock until the skin splits open. Then it wriggles out of its old skin and leaves it behind. A new skin is revealed underneath.

Prickly porcupines

Instead of hairs, porcupines have sharp spines that protect them from hunting animals. When porcupines sense danger, muscles in their skin tug on the spines to make them stand on end.

Blubbery bears

Polar bears have to survive in very cold temperatures. That's why they have a dense covering of fur that traps warm air like a thick blanket. A deep layer of fat under their skin also helps to keep in body heat.

Clutching claws

Cats have claws that are far sharper than any nails. In the wild they can use these deadly weapons to attack or pull apart the creatures they hunt. When a cat doesn't need to use its claws, it can pull them inside its paws.

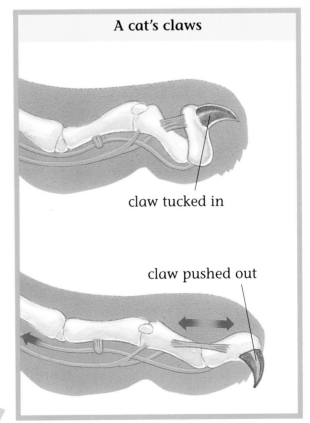

A cat's claws

claw tucked in

claw pushed out

GLOSSARY

albinos People whose bodies lack melanin, making their skin, hair, and eyes very pale.

allergy A person's sensitivity to something that may not harm other people—certain foods, plants, dust, or chemicals for instance.

anesthetic A drug, often given in the form of an injection, which temporarily numbs all or part of a person's body.

balanced diet Meals that include a wide variety of foods and contain all the nutrients and energy your body needs to stay healthy.

blackhead A small black spot on the skin caused by a blocked sebaceous gland.

blood vessels The many tubes that carry blood around your body.

camouflage Matching your appearance with your surroundings so you can hide.

cancer A disease that forms lumps, called tumors, which damage parts of the body.

carotene An orangey-red pigment found in some people's skin.

cells The billions of very tiny parts that combine to form tissues in your body.

collagen A protein that helps to make your skin and bones tough.

circulation The way blood travels around your body.

dermis The inner part of your skin, containing most of its working parts.

dominant gene A gene which overrules the effect of another gene.

elastin The protein in your dermis that makes your skin slightly stretchy.

epidermis The outer part of your skin.

evaporate To change from liquid to gas. Sweat dries by evaporating from your skin.

fibers Fine strands which make up many body parts, such as nerves and muscles.

follicles The small channels in your skin which your hairs grow out of.

freckles Small brown speckles on the skin, produced by patches of melanocytes.

genes Chemicals, found in every one of your cells, that carry instructions helping to determine how you look and develop.

glands Parts of your body that make juices.

goose pimples Tiny bumps that appear on your skin when your hairs stand on end.

heatstroke A condition people suffer from when they become too hot and lose too much salt and water through sweating.

homeostasis Your body's way of keeping conditions inside you finely balanced.

hormones Chemical messengers that tell parts of your body when and how to work.

insulate To trap heat inside, protecting against the cold outside.

iris The colored part of your eye.

iron An important nutrient, found mainly in red meat and leafy green vegetables.

keratin The tough protein that forms in the outer layers of your skin, nails, and hair.

lunula The moon-shaped white area at the base of each nail.

melanin The brownish-black pigment that helps protect your skin from the Sun's rays.

melanocytes Skin cells that make melanin.

moles Small dark spots on the skin formed by clumps of melanocytes.

nail bed The skin underneath your nail.

nerves Fibers that carry messages between your brain and other body parts.

numb Having no sense of touch or feeling.

nutrients The chemical substances in food that your body needs to survive.

papillae Nodules between your dermis and epidermis that form the patterns of your fingerprints.

pigment A chemical that determines your coloring.

pores Tiny holes all over your skin. Sweat comes out of them.

pubic hair Hair that grows between your legs when you become a teenager.

scar A mark left on the skin when a deep cut or bad burn has healed.

sebaceous glands Glands in the dermis that make oils which protect your skin and hair.

sensors The endings of nerve fibers, which pick up signals from your surroundings.

skin graft An operation to mend a large wound by growing new skin over it.

sperm A swimming cell, made by a man, that provides his baby with half of its genes.

subcutaneous tissue The fatty layer under your skin that helps to insulate your body.

sunscreen A chemical, usually in a cream or lotion, that gives your skin extra protection from the Sun's damaging rays.

sweat A salty, watery liquid that passes out of your body through your skin, helping you to cool down.

traits A person's features, such as hair color, height, and intelligence.

vitamin D A chemical that helps your bones to soak up and use calcium and other nutrients from your blood.

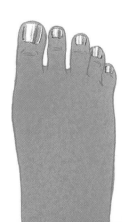

INDEX